SPIRITUAL STEPS

TO SURVIVING A TRIPLE-NEGATIVE

Diagnosis

CHEENA H. WRIGHT

Unless otherwise indicated all scripture references are from
the New International Version

Interior Design | Editing | Cover Design
DHBonner Virtual Solutions LLC
www.dhbonner.net

ISBN: 978-1973783893

Printed in the United States of America

I dedicate this book to *God,*

my heavenly Father, my Healer, my Refuge and Strength,
and my very present Help in trouble.

I also dedicate this book to **my mother,**

for all of her love and support.

And, to the honor of my late Aunt...
Shirley Ann Isley.

"Faith comes by hearing, and hearing by the word of God."

~Romans 10:17

Table of Contents

Foreword

A few years ago, while sitting at my desk on April 26th, I received a phone call from my sister Cheena; telling me a frightening story. *"I leaned against my cubicle and I felt a lump... and pain."* The words ripped through my mind and my heart in a way I was unprepared for.

Terrell and I drove to Greensboro to be with her, to pray with her, to wait with her. I remember days later, sitting in the oncologist's office, hearing this beautifully gentle man explain to my sister, his prognosis and his treatment plan.

We began to laugh.

Yes! We laughed at the plan of the enemy to dare challenge her faith, to dare war against her purpose in life, to dare and attempt to steal joy. WE sat through weeks of chemotherapy; laughing.

She was strong, when she had every right to be weak.

I learned that there is no distance I would not drive to hold her hand, because she is love, and faith, and sisterhood. Ultimately, God's promises reigned (as if there was any doubt) and they could find no more cancer in her breast or lymph nodes.

Her story is not one of victory – it is one of triumph.

Her faith brings her, not to a one time win over sickness, but to a life of triumph, as we are told to live in scripture. Her testimony is brilliant and glorious. She walked her steps, while caring for her two daughters. She just kept going, and going! God can do all things; her story is evidence of His power and His gentlemanly love.

She was stronger than I could've imagined.

I'm proud to have served her, and our God, through her journey. Read her book. Listen to the journey. Give thanks to God, who causes us to Triumph!

~Dr. Joynicole Martinez
Founder and CEO of the Alchemist Agency
Charlotte, NC

Preface

A Triple-Negative Breast Cancer diagnosis means that the offending tumor is estrogen receptor-negative, progesterone receptor-negative, and HER2-negative. This is from where the name "triple-negative breast cancer" is derived.

According to statistics, between 15-20% of breast cancers are found to be Triple-Negative. This type of breast cancer is known as an aggressive cancer and typically does not respond to receptor targeted treatment; however, it is responsive to chemotherapy.

Although this book may not address all possible actions, treatments, medications, precautions, side effects or interactions I had, it is my desire that this book will provide hope and reassurance. These are the spiritual steps that helped me survive the treatments, the emotional roller coaster, and the up and downs through the nights, while still being a mother to my daughters.

Nevertheless, for those of you who are faced with a Triple-Negative Diagnosis, I'd like to think of these spiritual steps as a way of providing you with an infusion of wisdom to support you and your family; as you navigate any cancer experience, with as much resilience and optimism as possible.   And, of course, I do advise with all matters concerning your health, that you consult a medical doctor or appropriate health care professional.

Confrontation with the word *breast cancer* is a searing inner experience that will weigh in on a woman's confidence. While writing this book, I went back over the sorrows, the pain, and the joys that have made me feel more alive today than I did eleven years ago. I hope that by sharing all of this, I will help you triumph in your own journey, as well.

Acknowledgments

To my beautiful daughters, Bionca M. Wright and Brandi M. Wright, who were the wind beneath my wings and who keeps my sail going. You are my two heartbeats; I could not have done it without you. Thank you for keeping a smile on my face, keeping laughter in the room, and understanding when mommy was not feeling her best; for trusting in God and knowing He would take care of us and not leave us.

To my mother, Sandra E. Headen, who had to relive those daunting words "Breast Cancer" after losing her best friend; her sister, years prior. Thank you Momma, for keeping a strong heart and not letting me see you cry. I know there were many nights you closed your bedroom door and cried yourself to sleep. You have and continue to be my inspiration, my motivation to be strong, and not give up! Thank you for keeping the refrigerator stocked with watermelon; the only thing I could eat and not get sick.

To my Brother, Terrell, and Sister-n-Love, Joynicole; you stayed by my side the whole time from the beginning of the diagnosis. You prayed and believed with me, took me to all my doctor visits, and accompanied me to my chemo treatments, so I would not be alone and have to drive afterwards. When it looked like I did not know what I was doing... you stepped in.

I want to give a special thanks to Demetrius L. Brown of *One Community, One Voice, One Vision*. From day one, you have supported the vision. Pastor Cassandra Elliott, thank you for nudging me to complete the process. Taurea Avant, for the wisdom you gave at the **Show Your Success Workshop** on writing the book. Pura M. Lopez, gracious para tu apoyo y siendo parte de mi primero libro.

Elder Desireé Harris-Bonner, thank you for listening to our heavenly Father. Hab 2:2 [NASB] says: "Record the vision and inscribe *it* on tablets, that the one who reads it may run. *"For the vision is yet for the appointed time; It hastens toward the goal and it will not fail. Though it tarries, wait for it; for it will certainly come, it will not delay."* Thank you for running with my vision.

To my silent sponsor, this all would not be possible for others to read, if it was not for your grace towards me. Thank you for believing in me, and encouraging me to finish the book, so others can read my testimony. I am truly grateful.

To Pastors Lee and Shonia Stokes; your support, love, encouragement, and the Word of Faith you taught, keep me rooted and grounded. It was the strong faith, you both shared with your testimonies, that helped me to activate my faith!

Prologue:
My Testimony Begins

January 2007

Hello Momma, how are you doing?

Momma replied, "Oh, me? I'm doing well."

So, after church last week, I was thinking about what Pastor said.

"What did he say baby?"

Well, Pastor was talking about renting, versus owning, a home. He mentioned owning property, and right now I'm in this beautiful house, but I'm renting it, and I was thinking...

Silence was on the line, as momma listened for what I was going to say next. I continued, *"I was thinking about buying my own house."*

"Great idea baby, when are you doing that?" momma asked.

I'm glad you asked. See, my plan is for me and the girls to move back home with you, to save money for a nice down payment.

Momma then replied, "Bring my grandbabies on home and stay as long as you need to."

Have you heard the saying, "If you want to make God laugh... tell Him your plans"?

You see, my plan was to move home to save money and buy a house, return back to what I and my daughters called "Home" since their father and I divorced in 2004. Not knowing that April 2007 would present a different type of plan; a different type of Life Plan!

Let me go back 4 months into time. September 2006, the week before my 35th birthday, I was at work having a conversation with my employees about the Mobile Unit that was coming to do free mammograms on site; sponsored by the company. Years prior, my Aunt didn't survive a breast cancer diagnosis. After her passing, doing self-exams was a normal thing for me, so I was excited about getting the mammogram done. I waited until my lunch period and stepped up on the mobile unit, ready to take this diagnostic test.

I completed the paperwork and the nurse called me back. She looks over the completed paperwork and said, *"Ms. Wright, I apologize, you are not 35 yet, so we will not be doing your mammogram today."* I told the nurse, *"I will be 35 in 7 days."* She replied, *"We will have to refer you to your doctor, so you can have it done after your 35. I apologize. I know it makes no sense, but you have to be 35 for us to complete the test."*

Feeling perplexed, I smiled, said "Thank You" and walked back to my desk. I did not think about the mammogram again.

Fast forward into 2007; after moving back home with momma, the girls and I were living life as normal. I was saving money for a down payment for my house, going to work, taking the girls to school, cooking us dinner, going to the park, going to cheerleading practice, going to dance practice, etc. One evening, Brandi (my youngest daughter) came to me and laid her head on my chest and asked, *"Mommy, are you going to die?"*

This caught me by surprise, and as I hugged her, I replied, *"Baby no, Mommy is not going to die. What made you ask me that question?"* She said, *"I just wanted to know, because we were talking about it at school".*

Now I had no idea who she was having this conversation with at school, nor why it was a discussion. But, the next couple of weeks showed me how *"From the mouth of children and infants God has ordained strength"* (Psa 8:2).

As I think back to that time, I realize that this was a warning from God of what was to come.

April 4, 2007

While doing a breast self-exam, I noticed a thick spot that didn't feel normal. At the time, I was going to school for Medical Coding, so it was nothing to have some medical books in the house; I pulled out a medical self-help book.

My monthly cycle was also going on, so to feel lumpy breast was normal, according to the medical book I had pulled out to read. The book advised to wait a couple days following the menstrual cycle and recheck the breast; because, during your cycle, the breast can appear lumpy, and there could be some discharge. If the feeling was still there, then contact your doctor.

I didn't immediately check my breast in 3 days. However, a week or so later, I was at work and I leaned against the cubicle wall. I felt this spot that presented some pain, so I immediately called my gynecologist and set an appointment.

April 18, 2007

I went for a clinical exam, where my gynecologist said he also felt what I was feeling and wanted to do a needle aspiration, to see if he could get some fluid out. Well, the needle aspiration did not work; my breast tissue was too dense for him to reach the spot. Concerned, the doctor had his nurse contact the Imaging Center for me to get a digital mammogram done.

Directly from the GYN office I went to get a mammogram.

Once I had the mammogram done, the nurse had me sit in the waiting room until the physician could read the test. While sitting there, I wasn't experiencing any type of anxiety; I was in no way concerned or worried. To me, it was all routine testing. So, I waited patiently for the nurse to come back and take me in the room to tell me, "Ms. Wright, it's nothing".

However, when the nurse called me from the waiting area, she asked me to come back into another room, because they wanted to do an ultrasound for extra testing.

After the ultrasound, I went back to a waiting room to wait again. Still... no type of worry crossed my mind. Instead, I was thinking about what time I would get back to work, what reports I needed to complete when I got back to work, and what else I had on my calendar "to do list" for the week. After about what seemed to be 30 to 45 minutes later, the nurse came to get me, and take me to see the doctor.

The doctor pulled up my films and showed me the spot. She said, *"Ms. Wright. Well, it is evident that there is something there, by the darkness in the tissue, as seen on the film. It appears to be a malignancy, which is common in African American women, like fibroid tissue. It is a perfect circle; if it were benign, it would be abstract in shape. I'm going to refer you to get a biopsy done to confirm this."*

The doctor left me with no worry, so going to have a biopsy raised no concern with me. I went back to put my clothes on, and headed back to work to finish out my day.

April 23, 2007

I arrived to have the biopsy done. After getting in my gown, the nurse took me into this cold room, with a medical table covered with sheets. She told me to lie down on my back and offered me a warm blanket to put over me. As I lay there, I looked up, and on the ceiling was a beautiful picture of flowers. I guess that is a calming mechanism. Then, the doctor came in, introduced herself, and thoroughly explained the biopsy procedure and that she would be numbing the biopsy area.

The biopsy felt weird; some pressure, but no pain. Then, it was over, and I was sitting up on the table. The doctor advised the results would be back within 24 hours.

Now, during the past 3 weeks, I had not allowed worry to attack my mind and I had been in prayer over my body. I had also chosen very few people to tell what was happening. I had talked to Rhue, my sister in Christ, explaining to her what was going on and asking her to be in prayer with me. I had also spoken to Pastor Katrina Williamson at church, who asked me if I was standing on any scriptures during prayer. I told her I did not know any specific ones, so she gave me a sheet called *"God's Word Is God's Medicine"* and out of the scriptures, she told me to pick several to meditate on.

So, for the next 24 hours, I went into prayer mode; meditating on Isaiah 58:8, Jeremiah 30:17, Psalms 30:2 and Exodus 15:26.

April 24, 2007

A Life Changing Eventful Day! I go back to the Breast Center to receive my biopsy results. The nurse had me to change into a gown and sit in a nice comfy room with a couch, tables, and a bookshelf. Now, this was not like the room I was in the day before. Soon, the doctor walked in and said, *"Hi Ms. Wright. It looks like cancer and we have you set up with an appointment to see a breast surgeon."*

My mind immediately went into Charlie Brown mode; everything sounded like "Wa wa wa... wa wa wa waaaaa!"

As she spoke, I began having an outer body experience.

I watched her mouth move, watched her get up walk across the room, and then walk back over to me with a white binder in her hand. While she talked, she handed me the binder with a picture that said "My Journey".

Now, I was saying to myself, "Why did she give me someone else's Journey Book with a page for appointments, resource pages, and more?" She also handed me a business card with a doctor's name on it, some informational pamphlets, and some other stuff.

The doctor was talking so fast, I had to stop her.

I told the doctor, *"Wait, Stop! Now tell me What It Is, How Big Is It, and How Do We Get IT Out!"*

She showed me a book that had diagrams of a breast and the name of the cancer was IDC (Invasive Ductal Carcinoma). After this, the doctor showed me a chart, sitting on the table, which had several different lump sizes and stated, *"Your lump is a Stage 2. The appointment you have with the surgeon will answer the plan of treatment for you."*

After the consultation, I returned to the dressing room, put my clothes back on, and before walking out I said, *"I Serve a MIGHTY God!"*

I smiled and walked out.

Spiritual Steps
to Surviving a
Triple-Negative Diagnosis

Prayer and Meditation

Prayer is when you talk to God;

meditation is when you listen to God.

~Diana Robinson

Prayer is a solemn request for help or expression of thanks addressed to God or an object of worship. **Meditation** is the act or process of spending time in quiet thought.

P rayer and Meditation was the first thing I started doing. Praying daily was a regular routine before even knowing about the lump. After hearing the words Breast Cancer, and knowing my aunt had passed from this same diagnosis, I decided that strategic and specific prayers were what I needed to stay the course. To keep my mind and heart in alignment, I had to meditate on scriptures like Isaiah 58:8, Jeremiah 30:17, Psalms 30:2, and Exodus 15:26.

After hearing the doctor say I would have 4 doses of Cytoxan and Adriamycin for 2 months, and then 12 doses of

Taxol for 3 months to complete my treatment, I prayed that I would have the mildest case of side effects from the chemo. One of my journal entries was, "I pray for the mildest case of side effects from the chemotherapy. I pray to my Heavenly Father that I am whole, healed, and my health shall spring forth speedily." I believed that Jesus died on the cross and rose from the dead just for me.

My words of meditation were:

"God has not given me the spirit of fear, but of love, joy, peace and a sound mind.

"No weapon formed against me shall prosper and every tongue that come against me in judgment they shall condemn."

"The Lord is my strength; He is the strength of my life."

Since the act of prayer itself has been associated with good health, quality of life, and lower levels of psychological distress in healthy people, it is just as important for those who are unhealthy. Prayer allowed me to offer praise and thanks, ask for help and guidance, affirm my faith, express my hopes and fears, and find solace.

Prayer and Meditation sustained me during my journey. My personal prayer time was simply me talking to God about everything. I would pray that God would give me more of a heightened awareness of His presence; to teach me how to recognize His voice. I would ask Him to speak to me so my life would not feel fragmented. It was time I spent developing a better relationship with Him.

I kept a prayer journal to write out what I wanted to talk to God about that was on my mind. It helped me to be quiet, and listen to God, for direction and understanding of the change I was going through.

My prayers included scriptures like Psalms 46:1 & 5 – *Lord you are my refuge and strength, a very present help in the time of trouble; I will not fear.* Psalms 34:19 - *Many are the afflictions of the righteous, but you Lord will deliver me out of them all.* Psalms 31:2 - *Lord deliver me speedily, be my rock of refuge, my fortress of defense.*

Pick a verse from Psalms or Proverbs that invites faith. After reading the verse, write it down, repeat it throughout your day, and then communicate this verse to God in your prayer.

Control Your Anxious Mind

Sometimes the best thing you can do
is not think, not wonder, not imagine, not obsess.
Just breathe, and have faith that everything
will work out for the best.
~ Robert Tew

Anxious Mind is characterized by extreme uneasiness of **mind** or brooding fear about some contingency: worried.

Philippians 4:8 (MSG) says, you'll do best filling your mind and mediating on things that are true, honest, just, pure, lovely, of a good report, of virtue, the best and not the worst, the beautiful, not the ugly, things to praise and not to curse. By putting these things into practice, God will work you into His most excellent harmonies.

While going through chemotherapy, controlling your anxiousness can be challenging. The chemo drugs have a huge impact on your hormonal system and the anxiety can be mild or bad.

I remember the very first time I had an anxiety attack.

The evening of June 12, 2007, I had taken some Tylenol for a headache that was a side effect from the nausea medicine I was on. My stomach was not doing well, so I put a pillow between my legs and my upper body, just to get to sleep. Well, while lying there, the panic attack started. I could hear my heartbeat, and it was beating a little slower than I was used to hearing, which caused the feeling of worry.

Then, as it became harder to breathe, I started crying. I had to get up out the bed and say my confessions out loud; praying before lying back down. I learned to pray continually for peace and a sound mind during these times.

The doctor prescribed a 0.5 mg tablet of Lorazepam for the anxiety as needed. I have never been a pill taker, so having to consume medicine for this was not easy. Then, it made me feel funny, so I stopped taking the Lorazepam and started paying attention to my body; playing back what I was doing before the attack started.

By doing this, I could manage the anxiety, without medicine. I quickly realized it was the chemo induced hot flashes that caused most of the anxiety. I chose not to take a bunch of medicine; only the necessary medicine to impact this tumor, so it could be removed.

Your mind is a battlefield. This is why the Word of God says in Philippians to *be anxious for nothing, but in everything by prayer and supplication, with thanksgiving, let your request be made known to God.* I had to turn that anxiety over to God and ask Him to take the feeling away. I had to calm my mind and remember that He would never leave me nor forsake me; that this was just a process that I had to go through and the reward was on the other side.

I could not let my mind get the best of me.

Two weeks after the chemotherapy treatments started, my hair began coming out. I was lying on the bed and reached up to scratch my head, and out came a plug of hair. The positive thing was that the plug came out in a spot I could cover up without anyone noticing.

By the third week more hair was coming out.

I was so glad I had gone looking for wigs prior to this. I was still working and had not told anyone I was working with about my situation, so this was overwhelming, and I was concerned that people would start talking about my wig.

OH... But God!

The short wig matched my complexion, and because I had already cut my hair in a short style, no one ever knew.

Mental anxiety lies on a spectrum and can always be channeled into something positive. When you feel anxious energy, just take a brisk walk and listen to the following scriptures in your mp3 player or on your cellphone.

John 14:27 (NIV) – "Peace I leave with you; my peace I give you. I do not give to you as the world gives. Do not let your hearts be troubled and do not be afraid."

Proverbs 3:5-6 (NIV) – "Trust in the LORD with all your heart and lean not on your own understanding; in all your ways submit to him, and he will make your paths straight."

Psalm 55:22 (NIV) – "Cast your cares on the LORD and he will sustain you; he will never let the righteous be shaken."

Colossians 3:15 (NIV) – "Let the peace of Christ rule in your hearts, since as members of one body you were called to peace. And be thankful."

Psalm 4:8 (NIV) – "In peace I will lie down and sleep, for you alone, LORD, make me dwell in safety."

Isaiah 41:10 (NIV) – "So do not fear, for I am with you; do not be dismayed, for I am your God. I will strengthen you and help you; I will uphold you with my righteous right hand."

Philippians 4:19 (NIV) "And my God will meet all your needs according to the riches of his glory in Christ Jesus."

Use Caution

"Every human being has, like Socrates,
an attendant spirit; and wise are they who obey its
signals. If it does not always tell us what to do, it always
cautions us what not to do."

~ Lydia M. Child

Caution is the care taken to avoid danger or mistakes. It is a way of behaving. **Caution** describes something that calls for careful action and the need to avoid risk, to put on guard.

After receiving a diagnosis of cancer, I had to use caution with my tongue. Proverbs 18:21(NKJV) tells us that *death and life are in the power of the tongue.* I had to make a choice every day to speak life to my body.

My Pastor (Lee Stokes) would say, *"Don't just allow anything to come out of your mouth. Set a watch over your mouth, and speak life, because you will eat the fruit of it. Stop letting your tongue testify against you!"*

When we are faced with a diagnosis that has the potential of taking our life, we tend to fall into a state of depression. Depression is a condition of mental disturbance, and a synonym for depression, is gloom. Gloom is partial or total darkness. The word says Life and Death is in the power of the tongue. Too many times we are quick to let our own words testify against us.

Caution your tongue.

I chose to speak life to my body daily. I would take my hand and place it over my breast and say out of my mouth, *"Every tissue, nerve, and cell must come into alignment with the word of God. By His stripes I am healed."*

I also made positive declarations over my life every day. I saw this as a temporary condition and I refused to allow it to get me in a depressed state of mind. I refused to walk around thinking 'Why Me Lord?' Instead, I would say, *"Okay Lord, what is it you want me to learn from this, and how do I tell others not to worry?"*

I had to caution my words, not only for myself, but for my daughters as well. My daughters watched my every move; therefore, it was imperative that I showed them God was in control. I could not walk around saying things like "I'm scared", "What am I going to do?", "Oh God, what about my daughters?" I made the decision to walk around saying, "My Praise is become my weapon", "I will not be defeated", "I will not be destroyed", "My body is healed", "I am more than a conqueror!"

Along with being cautious of the things I said out my mouth, I was also cautious about what I listened to, what I watched on television, and the people I talked with. It seemed like every commercial, on every station, or every other show, was talking about someone succumbed to cancer. It was like my mind was subconsciously noticing anything that had the word Cancer on it. Luke 11:34 tells us ***"Your eye is a lamp that provides light for your body. When your eye is good, your whole body is filled with light. But when it is bad, your body is filled with darkness."***

I'm sure you've heard the phrase, 'Eyes are the windows to the soul.' The things that we see, if not careful, can manifest in our hearts and minds and eventually turn into actions. What we hear and meditate on will also manifest into actions.

I found it hard at times to be around family, because they would remind me about my aunt who passed away from breast cancer. Thus, it was important that I surrounded myself with people who were Kingdom-minded and Kingdom-focused. Those who would speak positive things back into my life. What we hear and listen to, strongly affects the mind, whether immediate or later on; consciously or subconsciously.

Our thoughts and actions can either be in tune with God's intentions or not. Only by being in tune with God's intention will we ever know true fulfillment or happiness, while dealing with a diagnosis of breast cancer, or in life period. Prayer, discernment, and knowledge of God's revealed Word, is needed to discover how we can be in tune with His intentions (Ephesians 1:17-18).

Align your words with your Faith! Having faith and speaking against it, is like pouring oil in water, shaking it up, and looking baffled because it's not mixing. Speak into the atmosphere what you expect. Your words will form your world! What you say is your faith speaking!

Build a Support System

"Everything is energy and that's all there is to it. Match the frequency of the reality you want and you cannot help but get that reality. It can be no other way. This is not philosophy. This is physics.

~ Albert Einstein

Support System: A network of people that provides an individual with practical and/or emotional support.

B uild a strong system that will make you feel cared for, supported, and taken care of during this trying and vulnerable time. Hearing the words *"Ms. Wright, you have breast cancer,"* by myself, was a big pill to swallow. This diagnosis was the beginning of an incredibly difficult period for me and my family.

One of the most important steps I took to help me manage emotionally was to be surrounded by a strong support system. Ecclesiastes 4:9 says, *"Two are better than one, because they have a good reward for their toil."*

A strong support system requires positive energy. That positive support energy started with my daughters. At the time of my diagnosis, my oldest daughter was 9 years old, and my youngest daughter was 5 years old.

Following the first visit at the oncologist office, and processing all the things that I was about to face in the weeks to come, I decided to tell my daughters what was going on. After watching a video on chemotherapy treatments, and experiencing my hair falling out, I didn't want my daughters to be scared of their mommy.

So I let them know there was a lump in my breast, I let them feel the lump and told them the doctor said I needed to take medicine in order to get it out.

Now, at their age, they had no idea what it was or what it meant, and I was not sure why I was telling them to feel this spot. I let them know that the medicine I had to take would make my hair come out as well. My oldest daughter asked if my hair would grow back, while my youngest daughter hugged me. Brandi was the affectionate one; she would give an ant a hug, if she could figure out how to.

I had my hair stylist cut my hair short, so when the chemo treatments started taking a toll, I wouldn't wake up one morning with clumps of hair on my pillow and the girls afraid. Cutting it helped the girls get used to seeing me with shorter hair, and I bought a couple wigs for this phase of chemo treatments to wear.

The girls and I would find laughter in this process.

I remember, one day, when Brandi sat on the bed with my wig on, laughing.

[My youngest daughter, Brandi, with one of my wigs: 08/2007]

As I think back now, the girls never missed a beat while I went through this change. Their father and I had divorced back in 2004, but we remained friends and he was very supportive during this time for me with the girls.

Brian helped with caring for them, whenever I was not able to; coming by during the week and making sure they were doing well in school, that they had their homework done, picking them up for dinner, and taking them on the weekends. He also worked to ensure they still felt the love we both provided for them, even before this diagnosis came about.

My youngest brother Terrell and his wife (my sister in love) Joynicole, both ministers, were a big part of the strong support system. They were the very first people in my family that I decided to tell about the lump. I needed them to agree with me in prayer that my body was healed. Even though I just knew I was strong enough to handle what the doctor was telling me; I didn't take into account that having someone going with me to my doctor's visits was necessary.

Joy works in the medical field and she accompanied me to visit with the surgeon. Having her there, removed any nervousness I would have experienced, should I have had to go by myself. She also asked questions I had not even thought of. See, your mind can get very crowded with information, and you're hearing what the doctor is saying, but you do not really understand it all.

My very first visit to the oncologist was very overwhelming. Dr. M was very careful to explain how large the tumor was, as well as, if there was evidence of spread to my lymph nodes and other parts of my body. This is when I learned the type of breast cancer diagnosed called Triple-Negative. He said the cells did not have receptors for estrogen, progesterone or HER-2. So the anti-estrogen, progesterone, and HER-2 pills/treatment would not be helpful. The doctor could not give a prognosis prior to my having surgery. With this type of cancer cells, and to lower the risk of the cancer cells growing, he said I would need chemo.

Dr. M suggested two ways to start my treatment: 1) Have the lump removed and then do chemo, or 2) Do chemo to shrink the lump and then remove it. I opted for the second option; to do a treatment called Neo-adjuvant Therapy, where chemo is administered first to see if the tumor would react to the chemo, with hopes that it would shrink the lump. Although studies have shown cases where the tumor didn't react, to my favor, the tumor responded to the treatment and reduced in size from 2.2cm to 1.6cm, which was very significant.

My brother and sister-n-love would come with me to every doctor's visit. They would drive from Rocky Mount on each Thursday to pick me up and take me to my treatments. It was so good to have them there, instead of thinking about the needles and bags, and all that comes with this diagnosis.

They kept me laughing; finding ways to take my mind off of my current situation.

There are many different roles you will need the people in your support system to play. You will need people who will "just listen" when you need to talk; those who will give you good advice like your Pastors and those who will give you positive energy when you are not feeling your best. The team of doctors was very supportive. I recall the first visit with my surgeon; after Dr. I explained the type of surgery I would need, he asked if I had any questions. I asked him, *"Doc, do you know the words of prayer?"* He turned around with a big smile and said, *"Yes, Ms. Wright".*

That was the type of energy I needed around me. I was an active member at church, I sang on the praise team at church, and my church choir family was also a huge support. They stayed in agreement with me through prayer for no complications and total restoration of health.

It is important that you surround yourself with people who will be your gatekeepers; people who will be your prayer warriors and your cheerleaders. There are several support groups/programs through the American Cancer Society where you can get support from like the *Reach to Recovery* program, to connect with other survivors who are certified mentors, and *The Look Good... Feel Better* program, to boost your self-esteem while going through treatments.

Educate Yourself

In the war against breast cancer,
we have the ability to arm ourselves with knowledge;
education is a powerful tool. By taking action and doing
something positive, fear is replaced with hope.
~ Diahann Carroll

Educate: To provide with knowledge or training in a particular area or for a particular purpose.

E ducation is a process encouraged by God. God created our minds and designed it, so that a child who grows to maturity should increase in knowledge, wisdom, and skills (Proverbs 1:1-5). Education puts fears of breast cancer away and clarifies doubts. Many patients would rather avoid knowing about it; letting doctors deal with it, or just going with what the doctors tell them. Others find that exploring breast cancer is helpful in the process of recovery.

When my aunt passed away from breast cancer, I had no idea that there were several different types of breast cancer. It wasn't until I was diagnosed with triple-negative breast cancer, that I found it necessary to educate myself for various reasons: 1) What were my treatment options? 2) Was it genetic? 3) Will it return? 4) Will my daughters be impacted? and 5) What coping mechanisms were available to me?

Knowledge is a powerful, weightless, treasure you can take with you anywhere. Educating myself brought about my own awareness on understanding the basics of triple-negative breast cancer; myths, risk factors, and common treatments like surgery, chemotherapy, radiation, clinical trials, and genetic testing.

Through my research, I was able to confirm what the doctors told me at my visits. I found that triple-negative breast cancer is an aggressive type and likely to recur more than other subtypes of breast cancer. There are some very effective treatments for it as well, depending on the size of the tumor. According to the American Cancer Society triple-negative breast cancer affects all races; however, breast cancer in African American women is more likely to be triple-negative.

Education about breast cancer is clearly necessary. It will help you to be fully informed and you can ask more specific questions about your treatment plan. It will help you keep track of your progress and you will know more about the treatment methods the doctor uses. I was fortunate to have doctors who asked me questions about what I wanted to do and then told me the pros and cons of my decisions.

Dr. I asked if I wanted to conserve my breast, before he suggested I have a lumpectomy, which led me to ask him specifically the process of a lumpectomy. Never hesitate to ask the why, what, where, when, and how questions about your treatment plan.

Here are few questions to ask:

- Have you treated other people with Triple-Negative breast cancer?
- Is the cancer invasive or noninvasive? What stage is the tumor?
- What treatment do I need? What are the side effects? Are there ways to prevent or lesson the effects?
- Where can I find resources about Triple-Negative breast cancer?
- How do I preserve my fertility if I want to have children later?

Your team of doctors will get together and determine what your treatment will be based off the stage of the tumor and the grade of the tumor; meaning, how fast it may grow and/or spread.

Neoadjuvant therapy is the type of treatment I had. This type of treatment is chemo given as a first step to shrink the tumor. It helps the doctors see how sensitive the tumor is to chemo. After five months of neoadjuvant therapy, I had a lumpectomy to remove the lump and then 2 months of radiation therapy.

I wanted to become an advocate for triple-negative breast cancer, because through my journey, not many people I spoke with understood what it was. Many just knew it as breast cancer, but there are so many types of breast cancer. Research definitely helped me feel more secure with explaining what I was going through with concerned family and friends; enabling them to help me the best way possible.

Studies show that education on breast cancer helps to lower fear, tension, worry and confusion. So, take time out to educate yourself on the type of cancer that is diagnosed. A great source is www.cancer.gov

Adopt a Positive Attitude

Your living is determined not so much
by what life brings to you as by the attitude you bring to
life; not so much by what happens to you as by the way
your mind looks at what happens.

~Khalil Gibran

Attitude: A feeling or way of thinking that affects a person's behavior.

An important part of my coping with a cancer diagnosis, was recognizing that my emotions and feelings were all over the place. I had my 'up days' and my 'down days'. But, I attribute having a positive attitude as 100% of me being a survivor. Proverbs 15:13 says *"A merry heart maketh a cheerful countenance: but by sorrow of the heart the spirit is broken."*

To me, this scripture says it is okay to let people know about the diagnosis; however, I did not have to walk around looking sad. So, I maintained a happy countenance.

Here is a mathematical formula to the word: A-T-T-I-T-U-D-E would be 1+20+20+9+20+21+4+5 which equals 100%. Each of these letters is numbered by their position in the alphabet.

When diagnosed with breast cancer, people expect you to start moping around and looking hopeless. I recognized the need for a positive attitude while going through this journey, not only for myself, but more-so for my daughters. They stayed close to me, and watched my every move. It was important to me that I kept a happy countenance as much as possible in front of them.

I remember days when my emotions would get the best of me and I would go into the bathroom, and get into the shower, just so they couldn't see or hear me crying. After a prayer of release in the shower through my tears, I came out smiling, and the girls never knew. I refused to allow fear to control me and change my smile. I was determined not to pencil fear on my calendar. I had no time for fear, because I was focused on staying happy and continuing on with my life, as if this diagnosis never existed.

I have always been optimistic about things I've faced in life. Every Thursday, I had my chemo treatments and before sitting in the chair to get my port hooked up, I would go into the bathroom to pray. The nurses would always say, *"You have a pretty smile. Every time you come in, you're smiling."*

Maintaining a positive attitude helps with keeping a healthy outlook on life. The Mayo Clinic reports that positive thinking, leads to increased coping abilities, which reduce the harmful physical effects of stress. You can develop positive thinking by practicing positive self-talk and encouraging yourself.

I am thankful God showed me the positive in my situation. My thoughts remained focused on how everyday praise should continue to be in my mouth. One day, while driving down the freeway, I realized the season I was in while going through chemo treatments. It was during the summertime, and the weather was hot and humid, rain was very sporadic, and I thought how wonderful God allowed me to go through in this season. It could have happened during the winter months where colds, the flu, and other kinds of germs surfaced, that I would have been subjected to. I saw that time as God blessing me not to be sick and to stay healthy.

You control your attitude. Don't let a cancer diagnosis control your attitude. If you continually speak negative things, your heart will internalize those things, and your demeanor will be negative.

Decide to have a positive attitude; to speak positive things about yourself and the journey you are on. Speak positive affirmations daily like these that I used (and still use) to encourage myself:

- I choose to fill my life with joy
- I am fearfully and wonderfully made
- I shall live and not die
- I am the seed of righteousness and I have been delivered
- Nothing by any means shall hurt me
- By His Stripes I Am Healed
- I love and approve of myself
- All is well in my life
- I am purposed, predestined
- I Am Healed in Jesus Name
- I surround myself with positive people
- I Am a conqueror
- My body is healthy, My breast are restored
- I Am confident within my own skin
- I can do all things through Christ who strengthens me
- I shall live and not die
- I am inspiration
- I Am Happy
- I Am free to be me
- God is madly in love with me
- I Am LOVE

Write down affirmations that you relate to and then spend time in the mirror saying them. Do this every day to change your thinking. In the beginning, your mind will struggle as you repeat the affirmations; however, flow with the process and allow your mind to visualize the statements and impact your thoughts.

Maintain a Social Life

A healthy social life is found only,
when in the mirror of each soul the whole community
finds its reflection, and when in the whole community the
virtue of each one is living.
~Rudolf Steiner

Social Life is living in companionship with others, rather than in isolation.

A cancer diagnosis does not mean your social life has to suffer. Before I was diagnosed with breast cancer, I sang alto on the praise team at church every Wednesday night and every Sunday morning. After the diagnosis, I continued to sing alto on the praise team every Wednesday night and *both* services on Sunday. I didn't allow the diagnosis to stop me or change what I enjoyed; this was one thing that kept me going and maintained my hope.

I would have treatment Thursday morning... that evening I would go to choir rehearsal. On Friday, I would return to the hospital to get an injection called Neulasta. Neulasta is a prescription medication given approximately 24 hours after you receive chemotherapy treatment. It helps to reduce the risk of infection and provides support through your chemotherapy cycle. I would rest all day Saturday, and then on Sunday morning, I was ready to sing. I didn't miss a Sunday; even after having the port-a-cath surgery and the lumpectomy, I was still singing on Sunday.

During my season of treatments, I was still going to work. I was a manager at a credit card company, and my schedule was set up where I was off on Thursdays. So, I scheduled all appointments and treatments on that day. For my Neulasta shot, I would either go during my lunch break on Fridays or on the Saturdays that fell on a week I didn't have chemo treatments. Everything seemed to work out to allow me to still enjoy outings, while buffering against the social effects of cancer.

Maintaining a healthy social life helped me to not focus so much on the changes my body was going through. On the weekends the girls were gone with their dad, I would take myself to the movies. Since the chemo can impact your immune system, the doctor would suggest not being around a lot of people. So, I would go places at times when I knew there would be less of a crowd. Most days, I would have to wait until the sun went down, because the shine was very bright; hurting my eyes and making my skin ache.

In the morning, after dropping the girls off to school, I would head to the park and take a long walk; enjoying the morning before the sun started heating up the day. Exercise is something you want to sustain as much as you can. It can help lessen some of the side effects of the chemo treatments like depression, fatigue, or panic attacks.

According to cancer.org staying active with safe exercise will help improve how you function physically after treatments. You may not always be able to do everything you want, but maintaining quality of life helps increase levels of wellbeing, confidence, and faith.

Take Back Your Temple

"Let food be thy medicine and medicine be thy food."

~Hippocrates

Your Temple is an edifice or a dwelling place dedicated to the service or worship of a Deity.

C ancer cells really do act like armed bandits with no respect for your temple. Chemotherapy is a combination of drugs designed to stop the growth of the cancer cells. These drugs travel throughout the bloodstream in your body to destroy free radical cells that have/have not migrated from the breast tumor.

Unfortunately, while the chemo kills the proliferating cells, it also damages healthy white cells. Dr. M explained that the chemo would most likely weaken my immune system. Your immune system is what helps your body fight off disease. Knowing that the chemo would weaken mine, I refused to sit and just let it. Taking my temple back spiritually began long before the chemotherapy; however, now I needed to take action for the physical body to stay strong. 1 Corinthians 6:19-20 (NKJV) says *"Or do you not know that your body is the temple of the Holy Spirit who is in you, whom you have from God, and you are not your own? For you were brought at a price; therefore, glorify God in your body and in your spirit, which are God's."*

Nutrition was very important during chemo treatments; eating healthy, colorful, vegetables and fruits like watermelon, cantaloupe, grapes, and strawberries. I would have lots of watermelon, because the chemo changed the way most food tasted. Leafy green salads with broccoli and tomatoes was eaten either for lunch/dinner. I would drink plenty of water before each chemotherapy visit. I also drank Noni Juice for the healing agent of the fruit.

The company I worked for at the time had a full functional gym on site. My day began at 6:30am on the elliptical machine for 30 minutes, then walking the treadmill for 30 more minutes. I had to push myself to do this, but after starting, it was part of my daily routine, and my mind became conditioned to this, as this is what I had to do to recover and maintain my energy and confidence.

The enemy wants to destroy your health and steal your joy, BUT you have the power to control this illness, don't let it control you!

Activate Your Faith

*"Healers are spiritual warriors
who have found the courage to defeat the darkness of
their souls. Awakening and rising from the depths of their
deepest fears, like a Phoenix rising from the ashes. Reborn
with a wisdom and strength that creates a light that
shines bright enough to help, encourage, and inspire
others out of their own darkness"*
~Melanie Koulouris

Activating Your Faith is producing or involving action or movement; make active or more active.

Romans 10:17 says, ***Faith come by hearing and hearing by the word of God.*** Faith is trusting in, having confidence in, having belief in the word of God that says, "By His stripes, we are healed" (Isaiah 53:4-5) or "By His stripes ye were healed" (1 Peter 2:24).

This means, before this triple-negative diagnosis, I was already healed... and after this diagnosis, I am healed!

Faith can cause the supernatural power of the Spirit to come into play. Almost everyone knows what faith is; however, very few people know how to activate their faith when faced with a diagnosis that threatens the very life they live. Along with working through my emotional baggage, married in 1994, separated in 2001, and divorced in 2004, here comes this diagnosis called Triple-Negative Breast Cancer in 2007.

I mean come on, give me a break!

In order to start caring for my physical and mental well-being, I began looking into what I needed to do to activate my faith, while going through this new journey. When something is declared with a foundation of authority, power is released.

I had to claim this authority by declaring the word of God over my life. When we are faced with a diagnosis that has the potential for taking our life, we tend to fall into a state of depression. Depression is a condition of mental disturbance; gloom; partial or total darkness.

Psalms 23:4(AMP) says, *"Though I walk through the deep sunless valley of the shadow of death, I will fear or dread no evil for you are with me, your rod (to protect) and your staff (to guide) they comfort me."* Now the Word tells us that David WALKED through the valley of the shadow of death; it never said he stopped in the valley of the shadow of death.

A diagnosis of cancer will tempt you to stop and give up in that valley; however, this is where you have to activate your faith, get up and walk through, and while you are walking through, let God protect you. If you stop, you will always have in your mind the "What If?" I have too much work within me to complete for the Lord to let cancer stop me; I put all my faith in God! I knew that with a diagnosis like this, only God could see me through.

Back in July of 2007, Pastor Lee Stokes was teaching us about fulfilling our destiny, and he would say, *"You must use your faith to see the promises of God's purpose and plan fulfilled in your life."* Going through this journey was a part of me fulfilling my destiny.

The scriptures tell us that if we have faith the size of a mustard seed, we can move mountains. Another scripture says, **faith is the substance of things hoped for and the evidence of things not seen.** I would pray about this mountain called triple-negative breast cancer and I would, with my spiritual eyes, see me cutting this tumor out; telling this mountain to be removed, because God's word said I could!

Here are five steps I learned about activating my faith:

- **Ask** – You have to ask God for the things you desire.
- **Believe** – You have to accept God's word as truth without any sense realm evidence. You must

understand that your possibilities are defined by what you believe.

- **Confess** – You have to continuously speak in agreement with the word of God regardless of conditions and circumstances.
- **Demonstrate** – Your daily actions need to demonstrate that you are in agreement with your confession.
- **Expect**- You must live consistently in daily expectation of the manifestation of your faith desires.

As your faith is strengthened, you will see things start to flow as they will, and that you will flow with them, to your great delight and benefit.

So, diffuse the fear, and activate your faith!

Epilogue: Until Further Notice... Celebrate Everything

November 1, 2007

After five months of Chemotherapy, I had a Lumpectomy. Dr. I said they had removed the lump and cut out a clean margin around it; removing several lymph nodes.

All tests came back clear of any cancer cells.

The next phase was 33 treatments: Monday through Friday for 6 ½ weeks of radiation therapy. I was really hoping I would not have to take radiation therapy, but because of it being triple-negative, the group of doctors recommended it be done as a clean sweep.

January 22, 2008

...The last day of radiation treatment.

Dr. M covered the treatment plan, as well as, the reports from surgery and radiation. The one sentence Dr. M said still rings in my ear like it was yesterday.

"Well, your scans came back clear, your lymph nodes came back clear, radiation scans and MRI came back clear. Everything looks great. Time to go Live Your Life!"

• • •

Here is the takeaway; throughout this journey, I had no time on the calendar to pencil in fear, because it was already booked with Love, Joy, Peace, and a Sound Mind! Fear had no place in my life then, and still has no place to this day.

Don't misunderstand me, fear kept coming and coming, but I had no time for it! You must allow God to be in control of the situation. Put all your trust in Him, and He will direct your path through this diagnosis.

Exercise your faith, speak God's promises over your life, and watch Him work in your favor.

September 2007

September 2016

Affirming Scriptures

Psalms 8:2 (NIV) – Through the praise of children and infants you have established a stronghold against your enemies, to silence the foe and the avenger.

Isaiah 58:8 (NIV) – Then your light will break forth like the dawn, and your healing will quickly appear; then your righteousness will go before you, and the glory of the Lord will be your rear guard.

Jeremiah 30:17(NIV) – But I will restore you to health and heal your wounds' declares the Lord.

Psalms 30:2 (NIV) – Lord my God, I called to you for help, and you healed me.

Exodus 15:26 (NKJV) – For I am the Lord who heals you.

Psalms 46:1 (NKJV) – God is our refuge and strength, a very present help in trouble.

Psalms 46:5 (NKJV) – God is in the midst of her, she shall not be moved; God shall help her, just at the break of dawn.

Psalms 34:19(NKJV) – Many are the afflictions of the righteous, but the Lord delivers him out of them all.

Psalms 31:2 (MSG) – I run to you, God; I run for dear life. Don't let me down! Take me seriously this time! Get down on my level and listen, and please – no procrastination! Your granite cave a hiding place, your high cliff aerie a place of safety.

Philippians 4:8 (MSG) – Summing it all up, friends, I'd say you'll do best by filling your minds and meditating on things true, noble, reputable, authentic, compelling, gracious – the best, not the worst; the beautiful, not the ugly; things to praise, not things to curse.   Put into practice what you learned from me, what you heard and saw and realized. Do that, and God, who makes everything work together, will work you into his most excellent harmonies.

John 14:27 (NIV) – Peace I leave with you; my peace I give you. I do not give to you as the world gives. Do not let your hearts be troubled and do not be afraid.

Proverbs 3:5-6 (NIV) – Trust in the Lord with all your heart and lean not on your own understanding; In all your ways submit to him, and he will make your paths straight.

Psalms 55:22 (NIV) – Cast your cares on the Lord and he will sustain you; he will never let the righteous be shaken.

Colossians 3:15 (NKJV) – And let the peace of God rule in your hearts, to which also you were called in one body; and be thankful.

Psalms 4:8 (NIV) – In peace I will lie down and sleep, for you alone, Lord, make me dwell in safety.

Isaiah 41:10 (NIV) – So do not fear, for I am with you; do not be dismayed, for I am your God. I will uphold you with my righteous right hand.

Philippians 4:19 (NKJV) – And my God shall supply all your need according to His riches in glory by Christ Jesus.

Proverbs 18:21(NKJV) – Death and life are in the power of the tongue, and those who love it will eat its fruit.

Luke 11:34 (NIV) – Your eye is the lamp of your body. When your eyes are healthy, your whole body also is full of light. But when they are unhealthy, your body also is full of darkness.

Ephesians 1:17-18 (NIV) – I keep asking that God of our Lord Jesus Christ, the glorious Father, may give you the Spirit of wisdom and revelation, so that you may know him better. I pray that the eyes of your heart may be enlightened in order that you may know the hope to which he has called you, the riches of his glorious inheritance in his holy people.

Ecclesiastes 4:9 (MSG) – It's better to have a partner than go it alone. Share the work, share the wealth. And if one falls down, the other helps.

Proverbs 15:13 (MSG) – A cheerful heart brings a smile to your face; a sad heart makes it hard to get through the day.

Romans 10:17 (NKJV) – So then faith comes by hearing, and hearing by the word of God.

Isaiah 53:4-5 (NKJV) – Surely He has borne our griefs and carried our sorrows; Yet we esteemed Him stricken, smitten by God, and afflicted. But He was wounded for our transgressions, He was bruised for our iniquities; the chastisement for our peace was upon Him, and by His stripes we are healed.

1 Peter 2:24 (NKJV) – Who Himself bore our sins in His own body on the tree, that we, having died to sins, might live for righteousness, by whose stripes you were healed.

Psalms 23:4 (AMP) – Even though I walk through the sunless valley of the shadow of death, I fear no evil, for You are with me; Your rod to protect and Your staff to guide, they comfort and console me.

2 Corinthians 10:4-5 (AMP) – For the weapons of our warfare are not carnal, but mighty through God to the pulling down of strong holds; Casting down imaginations, and every high thing that exalteth itself against the knowledge of God, and bringing into captivity every thought to the obedience of Christ.

References

---

www.breastcancerpartner.com/positive_outlook.shtml

www.motivationalmemo.com/100-mathematical-reasons-for-developing-a-great-attitude/

www.biblegateway.com

www.mayoclinic.com/health/work-life-balance/WL00056

www.canceraustralia.gov.au/healthy-living/campaigns-events/world-cancer-day

About the Author

Cheena H. Wright, Author, Life Coach Speaker and Advocate of Triple-Negative Breast Cancer Awareness, is the founder of Triple Empowerment Network, 1000WomenInMotion, and also PINK4CHEE, Inc.

Cheena is a survivor of Triple-Negative Breast Cancer, and is an outstanding inspirational speaker, who connects with her audience through being transparent about her journey of Breast Cancer; sharing the steps she took traveling this journey and surviving this time of her life.

Cheena's portfolio consists of hosting a variety of events and conferences to inspire, empower, educate and to raise awareness in the community about Early Detection and Triple-Negative Breast Cancer. Events like, the 1st Annual Breast Cancer Survivor Gala, Golf Tournaments, 5K Races and Women Empowerment Conferences. Cheena is also a certified Mentor thru the American Cancer Society where she serves as a mentor for their Reach to Recovery Program.

Cheena has also served on several Executive Boards for Las Amigas, Incorporated a National Organization of Women. She has served as National Reporter, Regional Executive Board Recording Secretary and Local Chapter President. During her service Cheena started the initiative in the local chapter to donate Fleece Blankets to the Moses Cone Cancer Center in Greensboro, NC. The blankets were donated not just to Breast Cancer patients but to all cancer patients to be used during their chemo treatments. A National project called "Comfort of Love".

Cheena H. Wright has huge vision and passion that will impact the lives of many women all over the world. Her passion for educating all women about breast cancer prevention and taking their life back through education is an everyday mission for her. Cheena H. Wright attributes her survivorship to her faith and creating a platform for other women to share their journey of living and speaking life.

For booking, contact: **cheenahwright@gmail.com**

Made in the USA
Monee, IL
30 April 2025